Bitter Miles, Sweet Smiles

"Let's survive long distance relationship together."

Namrata Santoki

First Published in July 2022

ISBN: 978-93-5704-290-1

Price:

BLUEROSE PUBLISHERS

www.BlueRoseONE.com

info@bluerosepublishers.com

+91 8882 898 898

Cover Design:

Aman Sharma

Typographic Design:

Namrata Saini

Distributed by: BlueRose, Amazon, Flipkart

Contents

Acknowledgement

First and foremost, I would like to thank my soulmate, my husband, Dharmesh, who became my inspiration to write this book. He showed me the path to survive our long-distance relationship. So, I am really grateful to him that he also poured in some words for me through surprise letters that I have mentioned in my poetry collection and he allowed me to disclose them here. Moreover, he was there to support me throughout my book writing journey.

Then, my parents, my brother and my extended family who have always motivated me to keep writing. I thank them that they have been a great support to keep my pen moving on the pages.

Also, I would like to thank my friends. It's hard to name them individually here, as I have some friends who are my family and many friends who have simply crossed my path but gave a meaningful essence to my literary world.

Lastly, a big thanks to all the readers and couples out there. They have also been a great motivation to write this book specifically for long distance lovers and also in general when it comes to relationships. I am grateful that their eyes admired the essence of this context and are successfully holding this book in their hands today.

A big thanks to Blue Rose publishers for the smooth process and dedication.

Image credits (inside the book) : pixabay.com

Preface

Dear Readers,

We all know that relationships are wonderful if nurtured well. You as readers are here definitely because you would be in some kind of relationship. This relationship might have turned into long distance due to work or study or simply because you met your better half online. Whichever be the case, I am sure this book will give you some sort of relief from the stress build up due to the long distance relationship. I can tell this as I myself have been in a long distance relationship for about 2 years that too without meeting each other in person for the first time. This situation of being unable to unite was due to the pandemic in 2020. The time was quite tough, the pandemic, recession, anxiety, stress of not being with your loved one during these critical times. We did have arguments and disagreements, and that's normal in any relationship, added to this was the frustration of the unreachable distance between us.

I was residing in India and him, in North America. We knew it was getting more and more difficult but we had faith in our love and commitment. After this long time, when the first time I saw him in person, my rest of the senses awakened. Till that time, from a long distance we had just seen and heard each other and mostly felt each other's emotions by heart. The day we held our hands in person, it was the best moment of my life and I knew marrying this person would be wonderful.

Just finding a partner won't bring you satisfaction in a relationship, it comes by gathering the courage and surviving through all the phases of life.

I learnt this from my partner, Dharmesh, we have lived through ups and downs, happiness and sorrow, but, ultimately, he showed me the path of the relationship which had both bitter and sweet moments.

Any romantic relationship starts with a lot of fun, but over time we realize the differences, which have to be bridged together to make us focus on their core nature.

Nowadays, long distance relationships have become a part of modern love. A strong foundation for long distance or even close-by relationships, is patience, trust and love, to build an unbreakable bond. There are moments of joy and tears, but ultimately, they are worth it. Disagreements and arguments are just like the phases of the moon, which illuminates the dark nights and brings you closer despite its scars.

True love brings you peace in your partner's arms and into the depths of their eyes. Through all these, you take vows to spend a life together forever, and truly love the soul within, which never gets old.

This book simply compiles these moments and makes us conscious about them, which many of us will be able to relate and learn from. There is a lot of information available on the internet regarding how to overcome long distance relationships so I won't elaborate it here in my book. I have just tried to compile, in a very simple way, the phases of a long distance relationship which if survived bravely brings a lifetime promise to hold each other's hands through the hurdles and celebrate the beautiful love story sitting under the night sky in old age. I have shared my personal experiences through my journey of long distance and along with it some practical mantras for you to deal with your relationship too. This will give you a sense of relief that you are not alone facing the sorrow of a long distance relationship and everything is normal. One should always work on their relationship instead of breaking up.

The poems in between will help you soothe your long distance relationship journey. You'll take along some sweet memories and reminiscence about your time together with your partner. My purpose to write this book is to save the relationships that don't work out just because of the miles of distance between the partners. Also, to give you a good imagination of a lovely life after you make this long distance relationship work despite the odds. I hope this book caresses your relationship.

God bless everyone!

Namrata

Dedicated to

My Soulmate

Dharmesh Patel

Why do I write?

As the empty pages call me,
To pour my words on them,
With a smile on my face,
I ask myself, "Why do I write?".

My single ink pen,
Relishes as it swirls,
And paint on my words,
I ask myself, "Why do I write?".

In the morning glory,
And in the night's silence,
Or in the intricate hustle of the day,
I ask myself, "Why do I write?".

When my inner instincts lighten up,
They set my vision straight,
To lead me to the empty pages,
I get my answer to, "Why do I write?"

To embrace my solitude,
And to appreciate the silence,
I can give words to my emotions,
That is why I write....

In the morning dew,
Chirping birds sing a lyrical verse,
My words flow with its melody,
That is why I write....

In the crashing waves on the shore,
With seashells on the sand,
I leave the footprints of my memories,
That is why I write....

As I sit on the river bank,
The Golden fireflies,
Illuminate my soul,
That is why I write....

In some phases of life,
When I am bewildered,
The words give me moment of pause,
That is why I write....

To cherish the magnificence,
Of the nature and its creations,
I feel gratitude towards God almighty,
That is why I write....

Decision of Stepping into LDR.

The first step is you are landing into a long distance relationship due to study or work which might be several miles away for a short or long duration. The decision to be in a relationship despite knowing that you and your partner are distant is the first stepping stone of a successful relationship. Yes I am saying it is successful. Believe me, you didn't refuse straightaway or didn't consider your relationship should necessarily have a physical presence. This shows your willingness to be in a LDR and give it a chance to work out positively.

A True Instance:

Me and my partner met each other on a matrimonial site and just became friends first. We just liked to talk about science, personalities, ethics, spirituality and God. Both of us were unclear about our future prospects but within a few days of our talk, we knew that the matrimonial site was showing the correct match for both of us. We didn't know when we would meet each other in person, not even a tentative date, as we were many time zones apart that too in a pandemic.

Mindful Mantras:

- Accept the fact that it would definitely be difficult and uncertain. No long distance relationship is easy.

- Gather the courage to gulp the overwhelming emotions of distancing from your partner. (Have a lot of water.... It does help with the anxiety)
- Always bid goodbye with a smile on your face. The last image of yours in your partner's mind is very crucial. Cry beforehand as much as you want but when leaving, SMILE. It will make you feel good when you will sit and remember the smiling faces of you and your partner during your last meeting.
- If you meet online, you have to take responsibility for how the relationship progresses and commit to yourself to have patience understanding the person from a distance. (Make sure about the genuineness of the profile of the person online)

Hello

It starts from a hello,
A greatest adventure,
From a simplest conversation.
The mind whispered,
In the nervous body,
"Is he the one?"
The heart murmured,
"Keep going dear,
The destiny shall lead,
The path will be clear."

The Butterflies in Stomach

Changed my social media display picture,
Just to get her compliment.
Uploaded an old photo on Instagram,
Just to get her likes.
Sent one more wish on her birthday,
Just to get another "Thank you".
Watched her "last seen" again and again,
Just hoping she will text first today.
The heart whispered
"One more message please."
The shrewd mind interrogated,
"Where are these butterflies coming from?"

The Change

When you get into a relationship, you are aware that you are in a totally different world. You see changes in your emotions, behavior, and daily schedule. When in a healthy relationship, you glow with confidence and happiness. You and your partner are two different individuals with different tastes but since you are together you must also be having some similarities. In a relationship, you are trying to merge yourself with your partner which is a slow process. So when you understand that this is the case in a normal relationship, the same thing applies to a long distance relationship.

When you suddenly get distanced from your lover, or are already in a long distance relationship, there would definitely be some more differences added to it. Both partners would be getting accustomed to this change differently. When in a LDR both the partners should respect each other's emotions and be there for each other.

A True Instance:

For us, our relationship started in two completely different worlds. Everything was distinct between us, the time zones, choices, professions, and work schedules. Only the core belief of love was similar between us. We had to cater to each other's need for love and then everything else fell in place. Yes, our souls merged over time.

Mindful Mantras:

- Be prepared mentally that a drastic change would occur as soon as you are in a LDR.
- When you respect the change, you try to respect your partner's space and emotions.
- When you patiently understand your partner's feelings you make better decisions or plans on how to accustom to the changes.
- Initially, you are more dependent on your partner emotionally as you have just distanced from them and that's completely normal. Just give it a time and don't let the emotions engulf you. Remind yourself that this is not the end of the world. The sad feeling would soon pass and you would be fine within a few weeks.
- When you are getting into a LDR as you met online, everything would seem to work out initially, but gradually the constant pain in your heart of not being able to meet your lover makes you see the changes in a negative way. Remind yourself to view the relationship with a positive perspective and whatever you feel is due to the gap caused by the distance of miles and not between your hearts.

Bridge the Differences

Her days were his nights,
Her smile was his remedy,
Her voice made his heart beat,
Her passion was his dream.

His morning texts and her night calls
His success was her happiness
His care and her prayers,
His commitment and her promises.

In dark and light,
Through ups and downs,
Their only goal was
To bridge the differences.

A Healthy Habit

A happy relationship is made up of healthy partners. The "Healthy" here means physically, mentally, emotionally and spiritually. To create healthy relations partners get used to each other and get into a habit. To understand this, you need to know the two concepts that work here. Firstly, you are trying to pick up your partner's habit for a better change. Second is that you as partners are becoming each other's habit. Either way you are gradually merging yourself with your partner like I mentioned earlier in the last chapter. Let's have a look at my example to understand this better.

A True Instance:

My partner attended the Sunday assembly and before meeting me, he sometimes couldn't concentrate on it and got distracted. When we got into a relationship, he got to know that I like the spiritual teachings but couldn't attend them due to some reasons and since then he started paying attention to it so that when we called each other he could tell me about the teachings on the phone. We have got into a regular habit of doing this together every weekend over the phone. We picked each other's habits for our betterment.

Second instance is that there hasn't been a single day in our two years of LDR that we didn't talk over the phone. The mood checking and what food we had for lunch/dinner was basic and we always paused and took those 5 minutes to call and check on each other. This way we have become each other's habit.

Mindful Mantras.

- Try to know your partner's daily schedule and mood patterns. It is important in a LDR as you aren't physically present. This basic love and care that you can give each other from a distance can reduce infidelity to a great extent.
- Take out a few minutes to check in with your partner. A simple "How are you doing today?" Or "What was special for dinner tonight?" can mean a lot in a relationship.
- Pick your partner's good habits. This way you would be making a healthy relationship with a healthy future. (Make diet charts together and track them, exercise and do yoga together on video calls)

Which of your partner's habits have you decided to pick? Write it down.

You:______________________________

Your partner: ______________________________

The Good Habit

When the sun rises,
My heart opens with her warmth,
Another day with vivid hopes,
Compiled with new challenges.
She comes around with novel ideas,
Lifts me up to embrace the chances,
And taught me to love from distance,
That's how she became my good habit.

When the sun sets,
Gradually the life settles down,
But, my enigmatic thoughts awaken,
Questioning my mere existence.
He comes to make my soul alive,
Defining the purpose of life,
And holding my hand from distance,
That's how he became my good habit.

Doubts and False Anticipations

When we talk about long distance relationships, apart from the distance, comes the drawback of difficulty in trusting. Not having your partner by your side and knowing him/her, enjoying with friends might sometimes create some doubts in your mind. "Would he be making new friends who are girls?", "Would she be wearing improper outfits and going to parties with male friends?" These kinds of thoughts start clustering your mind. This might lead to a situation of misunderstanding between you and your partner which can be a biggest setback in your LDR as it's a matter of trust.

With doubts also comes false anticipation. Human minds tend to create imaginary situations a lot. You might start thinking about everything wrong your partner could do just because you aren't together in person. This false anticipation can even give a panic attack to some people. Sometimes you doubt your partner and sometimes you get into false anticipation just because you couldn't communicate properly with your better half.

A True Instance:

My partner always used to text me in the morning, that is, his night, as we lived in different time zones. There has been a time in our lives, when he wasn't able to text me in the morning. Generally, sooner or later he does wish me in the morning but not on that one day. This did give me doubts about what could possibly make him busy at night that he couldn't text me. I also created false anticipation in my mind that he must be with his friends partying. Added to it, he wasn't reachable on his phone. Panic attack! ....Turned out after 15 minutes I got morning text along with an emoji of cooking food as his roommate was sick and his phone battery was down. From there on he shared with me his daily schedule and without fail texted me if he was out and gave me a tentative time he would call. Also he checked on me undoubtedly whenever he was out with his friends.

Mindful Mantras:

- Talk openly about your insecurities with your partner. (Get those little devils of jealousy and suspicion out of your mind)
- Make a deal to let each other know what are the plans for your weekends beforehand. Avoid jumping into situations such as immediate outing plans and not getting a chance to inform your partner. (A small text hardly takes 10 seconds)
- Share a common calendar where you are putting your upcoming activities. This builds a sense of trust as you are including your partner into important events.
- Try to know and talk about their friends and roommates.
- Instead of false anticipation, call your partner and talk it out. Have alternate contacts to reach out to avoid panic situations.
- Frequent gestures of love and appreciation helps build trust in any relationship.

Have you been through a similar situation of doubts and false anticipation? If yes, then you know what you have to do to figure it out peacefully. What are you waiting for? Make a plan with your partner to avoid situations of doubts and fight your little devils of suspicion.

Trust

The five-letter word resembles,
To walk the path of love,
With closed eyes.
It is the ultimate power,
To hold the deepest secrets,
And the wildest fears.
Engrossed in honesty,
It binds two hearts,
That resides miles apart.

Virtual Time

Virtual time is a necessary part of a long distance relationship. It doesn't imply just the video calls that you have with your partner. It defines the quality time that you spend with your partner doing activities virtually that you might be doing in person. This is essential for maintaining the sparks in a long distance relationship. This would make you miss your partner less as you try to create a situation like you are together.

A True Instance:

Our personal favorite was watching series and movies together every weekend. He also takes me to beautiful places whenever he goes on an outing. We have seen the sunsets on the beach together just by video call. Believe me it's a wonderful experience.

I shared my long distance virtual dates idea with one of my friends who actually isn't in a long distance relationship. They stay in the same city and meet frequently. Since she heard my idea, they have started visiting different restaurants once in a while and have virtual dates. They really enjoy this as they find it exciting to discuss the menu online and eat together thinking your partner is right beside you. She told me that the virtual date idea really makes them more excited to meet each other in person. They consider this habit healthy for their relationship.

Mindful Mantras:

- Schedule virtual time. Ask your partner about their wishes and discuss yours too with them.
- Watch movies, cook, read your favorite book and exercise together. Play online games, solve a relationship questionnaire together. Most importantly pray together.
- Virtual dates are amazing but generally underrated. Get into the excitement of trying new things in a relationship.

To give a kick start to your meaningful virtual time, let's list out a few activities that you want to do together this week. Later, you add some more different activities according to you and your partner's wishes. Write it down and share it with your partner, it's important to write as it gives you a feeling of dedication.

- ____________________
- ____________________

Gift of Love

Be the Romeo, to my Juliet
I'll conquer the mountains,
To hold your hand,
Till we lie on deathbed together.

Be the Jim to my Pam,
I'll be your best friend first,
And wait for the good things,
Until we love fearlessly.

Be the Noah to my Allie,
I'll chase my heart,
And fight the odds,
To grow old with you.

Be the Edward to my Bella,
I'll absorb the poison,
Let it rush into my blood,
To love you for a thousand years.

Intense Missing

Missing makes the love stronger. Missing your lover intensely is a basic sign of a long distance relationship and it makes your love deeper. When you miss your partner, you try to appreciate whatever quality time you get together and crave for their presence. This itself is a sign that love grows with distance. Partners value each other's presence in their lives.

A True Instance:

Whenever my partner and I miss each other, we leave a message on the phone. This way the person who is in the phase of intense missing vents out his/her feelings and the partner could do something to lift up the mood of his/her lover. This works both ways and it is a healthy way to deal with overwhelming emotions of a long distance relationship. When he isn't available I read a self-help book, listen to music, go for a nature walk, and watch the photos captured with my partner).

Mindful Mantras:

- Take care that you don't spend the whole day talking about missing your partner. It could ultimately make both you and your partner disappointed.
- Get a backup plan. Your partner won't be available whenever you miss him/her. Devise your own plan of what to do to overcome missing your partner.

- Missing your partner can sometimes lead to frustration and fights, so watch out your emotions and think to calm yourself down and also try to understand your partner.
- Thinking about how wonderful time it was when you were close together can make emptiness more intense for some people. So I would suggest looking forward to your next meeting and talking and visualizing more of the future with your partner.
- Give little surprises. Send a gift online as this will help minimize the pain of missing your partner.

So, have you decided what to do when you miss your partner? Have you got your backup plan if your partner is not available at the moment you are going through an intense missing phase? Write down three things that you would love to do alone until your partner is available for you.

1. ______________________________
2. ______________________________
3. ______________________________

Miles Apart

Sitting here thousand miles apart,
Away from the perception,
But my skin soaks the same moonlight,
And I confess looking at the starlit sky,
That "I miss you".
I might neither have social media post,
"Best lover ever",
Nor will I need to show our butterflies of love to the world,
But with the glance of your eyes,
I can tell that "You miss me".
We yearn for a glimpse,
As our hearts keep longing,
For a special moment,
To embrace each other,
With the beauty of meeting.

I Hear your Heartbeats in my Dreams

In the serene night,
When the moonlight shines,
Where the stars glistening bright,
Adorning the sky,
I hear your heartbeats in my dreams.

In the night blooming cestrum,
As I curl in the petals,
And the fireflies hover,
Enlightening the beauty,
I hear your heartbeats in my dreams.

You spin me around,
To the dancing grace,
The eyes shimmering luster,
The moon showering its glim,
I hear your heartbeats in my dreams.

The heart sings songs,
Of merry and love,
To deepen the slumber,
With a picture of yours,
I hear your heartbeats in my dreams.

And in your arms,
As you glance at me,
The satisfaction smiles,
And the beats synchronize,
I hear your heartbeats in my dreams.

Disagreements, Arguments and Frustrations

Disagreements are an unavoidable part of a relationship. A relationship is a bond between different individuals having different opinions about finances, intimacy, or something as simple as house chores. These disagreements often turn into arguments. Some of these arguments can also go long term. This builds up frustration in partners and it can have a devastating impact on the relationship. Added to it the exasperation of long distance and being unable to be together to sort out the matter is even painful. I am not saying to not argue at all, but the deal here is to learn the right way of arguing. Devise a way to communicate, time out and clearing the issue together.

A True Instance: Despite spending a lot of time together we still have arguments. In our case, we had a lot of arguments earlier and over time they have decreased a bit. Maybe because we learnt the time - out concept. While discussing something, if we get into an argument, my partner just tells me to give him a few minutes to drink water and have a walk in the cool air outside. Initially, I didn't really like this idea of my partner, like "How can he isolate me in such a situation?". I observed over time that not letting him vent out his feelings and resisting his time-out was creating more frustration. So now when we both get angry, I let him speak out what he feels, let him go for a walk, and when he comes back, he has a cooler mind, clearer solutions to our issue and often he comes with a "Sorry'" and "I love you".

Mindful Mantras

- Devise a healthy way of arguing. Give each other a chance to express their opinion.
- Set some boundaries to avoid abusive arguments, like no name calling, no swearing, no insults, etc.
- Have a time-out concept. Respect your partner for taking a few minutes to gather his/her emotions. Don't cut the phone on your partner's face, ask permission to leave for a moment. This is most important in a long distance relationship and it's a sign of respecting your partner even in the tension of argument.
- Don't let any argument stretch long term. An argument settled in a short time with love can prevent ruining your relationship. Try to express your love for your partner so that you go to bed in peace.
- Always remember, Love is more valuable than ego. Love can recreate any relationship, an ego will just destroy any relationship. So win and satisfy your love and not your ego.

So what are your plans when you get into an argument? What is the first thing that you would do when you realize that the tension is continuously building up between you both? ________________

Then what are the changes you would make in your mood, or what would you tell your partner to discuss in a more mature, healthy way? _____________

Worth my Tears

I slide into the heavy dusk,
As sorrow entangled,
The opinion fight,
The disappointment,
The hurt,
The pain,
Of seeing you with watery eyes,
In remorse,
In sadness,
But you are worth my tears.

Bitter Sweet

That quiet frosty night,
I sat beside the firewood,
Warming my frozen skin,
To the deepest layer.

A mail arrived at the doorstep,
I stood there with starry eyes,
The choicest chocolates,
From a distance apart.

Well, was it the dessert,
That made me charm again?
Or the sweet moments,
That follow the unpleasant ones?

Filling the lusciousness in my body,
Originating from my lips to my mood,
With a message to embrace,
The bitter sweet memories of our lives.

Communication

When we have just taken a look into arguments and misunderstandings that can arise in a long distance relationship, (or any close-by relationship), it's necessary to talk about communication. Now communication doesn't only mean the verbal act of delivering words in a precise way so that the relationship works smoothly. Communication is also the tone of speech, the body language, hand gestures and facial expressions. These little elements combined with genuineness, internal feelings and love have a big impact on how you communicate with your partner. When you love a person just by the simple words you can identify the tension between you both, or by a few gestures of love, you can understand the happiness of your partner. So communicating includes a respectful way of placing your opinions that can build a trustful relationship. In a LDR, communicating properly is inevitable as a major part of your time is online.

A True Instance:

We have set some rules to communicate better, listening to each other's opinions, reasons for disagreement and arriving at meaningful conclusions. When we feel that discussing some issue could lead to deeper arguments, we end the discussion for some time. Thereafter, I write an email or a letter to him stating my feelings, what I expect from him and where we went wrong. This way we are patiently able to listen and communicate our feelings.

Mindful Mantras

- Never give silent treatment. The long distance relationship is chiefly based on communicating online and the silence only builds up tension between partners.
- Have alternate ways of communication like writing an email or letter to express your hard to deliver feelings.
- Listen first, to be listened to. Communication is a two way process.
- Don't leave any topic undiscussed/half discussed as it can build resentment amongst partners.
- Care for each other. Caring is also a way of communicating the feelings of love and it many times helps partners to develop mutual respect and trust. This will ultimately help you open up your feelings or speak your heart out with your partners.

What is the alternate way of communication that you would use to discuss your feelings in the moment of tension? ____________________

If you disagree to a point, what's the best negotiation that you can arrive at? ______________________

If still not arrived at a decent agreement, write down points of pros and cons about the topic on a paper and decide accordingly. Write down separately for each of you.

Pros ________________________________

Cons________________________________

(I would recommend you to write down wherever there is a blank as writing down creates a positive impact on your brain and helps you make better decisions)

The Key to Relationship

Communicate,
Good or bad things,
Think with mind,
Speak with heart,
It's a key to understanding.

Communicate,
To build trust,
To raise faith,
To share the honest feelings,
It's a key to the locked emotions.

Communicate,
About fights,
And disagreements,
Through the shadows of sorrow,
It's a key to sustaining the dark times.

Communicate,
To listen,
And be listened to.
Be best friends first,
It's a key to a valuable relationship.

Consistency

Consistency in a relationship is essential and is described widely as sticking to your partner with actions of care, honesty, love and support over and over again. Loving is not a one day act and is a continuous process. Long distance relationships often lose their consistency simply because it's difficult to face those gloomy emotions for a long time. Also partners have to keep reassuring that their better half is also in a joyful mood that too from a distance and very few have this skill to endure the miserable days and bring happiness on each other's face.

A True Instance:

When I met my partner he was a master's student in North America, along with it he had a part time job and a loan on his head. After a few months the pandemic struck and it disturbed the whole world. I knew that we were there for each other but it was a real test. He was extremely stressed about the situation. He had to leave his part time job due to the pandemic. He started studying hard and applying for jobs in his field, as a software developer. He got back pain and was diagnosed with sciatica and had to visit a physiotherapist. He told me that he was a complete mess and I should look out for better options as a life partner as he wants a good life for me and doesn't want me to get into his life troubles. I didn't listen to anything. I just advised him to share the online calendar with me and tell me everything that he wants to figure out in his life. I organized his schedule on the calendar. He made some changes if he felt like and distributed time for study, interview preparation and actually applying for jobs. I had my own job but I became his "personal assistant" (just a funny way he used to refer) for managing his schedule. He spent two months only studying and one week of applying for many IT jobs and within a week of his graduation, he got his job. He had worked in India for two and a half years but this was his first job as an immigrant software developer. We never failed to plan together and pray together. He got his back problem fixed in the next couple of months. In about 6 months he paid back his student loan. We didn't leave any reason so that he could feel I deserve someone better. Everything falls in place if you are determined to work towards it. According to me, consistency has been the biggest reason for our successful LDR.

Mindful Mantras:

- Be honest and clear about your actions. For example, If you can't receive your partner's call or give valuable time for a day, apologize and communicate about the reason and try to make up for the lost time.
- Respect space. Partner's should take their "me time". Being in a long distance relationship, self care and space are necessary and one shouldn't underestimate it. Talking over phone all day won't make up for the distance between partners but it could actually create burn out.
- For consistency, it's necessary to take care of each other's dreams, wishes, hopes and space. Also, there should always be a desire to support your partner.

- Try something new, as it keeps the spark alive in a relationship.
- Difficult times are like phases of the moon, the dark time does not stay for long and slowly brings the light of full moon in our lives every once in a while. The moon constantly follows this pattern.
- Love is a continuous process. If love is true, distance isn't capable of diminishing it, love only grows when true lovers are apart.

The Phases Of Moon

The beautiful moon,
The reflection of heart,
Showering the moonlight,
On the silent souls.

In the clear sky,
As the full moon shines,
Being a great listener,
As the solitary souls talk.

Some couples making promises,
To catch a sight of each other,
Separated distance apart, united by moon,
Some just sit under it, in a lovely pose
Enjoying the beauty of the dark night.

From waxing to waning crescent,
Into the new moon on fortnight,
When the dark night surrenders,
Teaching us the gradual transformation.

As the new moon is reborn.
And when it turns into,
A little larger, brighter and red,
We worship the creator,
As we see the blood blue moon.

And as the moon and sun chase each other,
Never meeting though,
But as they converge,
Appears the wonder of eclipse,
Hiding the light, once in a while....

Prepare for your next/first Meeting

Long distance is all about longing to meet your partner in person. Making plans about your next meeting with a partner keeps you going in a relationship. You are excited about all the things you want to do together when you meet. For that you can design your personal itinerary.

If meeting your partner for the first time, you would be filled with nervousness and excitement. You should discuss your nervousness, fears and boundaries beforehand. It's completely fine for the first meeting and both the partners should respect each other's apprehension.

A True Instance:

When me and my partner were talking before meeting, it many times involved imaginary meeting scenarios. We used to imitate it on video calls that might help us be less nervous when we meet. I did talk about my fears and insecurities. We shared our wishes and choices, and planned our meeting accordingly. My partner is a quite organized person when it comes to planning. He likes to explain everything to me with a flowchart and he made one, which included everything, a whole plan from the first day at the airport to the last day. This brought clarity about finance and a decent plan to utilize the time we got together at its best.

Mindful Mantras

- Plan your next meeting, the things to do together, the places to visit, and the fun activities. Most importantly plan your finances together (flights, vacations, etc), it's necessary for a healthy long distance relationship.
- If you are meeting for the first time, ensure your safety. It's better to meet in a public place or at home with partner's family.
- Respect your partner's hesitations and boundaries.
- For the first time, prepare yourself mentally about slight variations you might see in your partner than on the video calls. The feelings, love, attachment are important and it's all that matters at last.

Have you made plans for your first meeting/next meeting? If not, what are you waiting for, start it today. It doesn't matter if you don't even know a tentative date, what matters is to plan for a moment when you both are finally going to be together.

The Wait

From,
Waking up to sunrise alone,
To,
Watching the sunset together,
Trust me,
The wait will be worth it.

From,
Unfolding the long letters,
To,
Holding your hand in person,
Trust me,
The wait will be worth it.

From,
Collecting the winter blossoms,
To,
Cherishing the divine springs of love,
Trust me,
The wait will be worth it.

From,
Craving for your one look,
To,
Counting down the days to meet you,
Trust me,
The wait will be worth it.

Important Milestone

Years passed by,
As the earth revolves on its axis,
The old one leaves,
And the new is celebrated,
The wait is finally over.

Months passed by,
Counting each leaf of the fall,
Snowflakes of the biting winter
And the wonderful blossoms of spring,
The wait is finally over.

Days passed by,
From each cheerful morning,
To the moon that peeks in silent night,
Whispering your messages from distance,
The wait is finally over.

Hours passed by,
With each ticking second,
I am more near to you,
United today, by patience,
The wait is finally over.

Now here I stand,
Looking into your eyes,
Your smile, your touch,
Your warm welcoming arms,
Together we say, " We made it,
The wait is finally over."

Finally Hand in Hand

The final moment when your distance would actually make you feel closer is the day you finally meet your partner. The nervousness, racing heart, happy tears, a lot more overwhelming emotions that you fix in your mind's memory box so you can cherish it later.

A True Instance:

Me and my partner were talking frankly and were very sure about our relationship online. I had set my boundary that it would take some time for the transition of our relationship from on screen to off screen. We had agreed on some terms on the phone that we might appear a bit different than what we seem on video calls, but it won't be something unacceptable. Our hearts and feelings would be the same and that's what matters.

On the day of the meeting, I was getting goosebumps and we both had upset stomachs. He traveled to India and the next day, I traveled to his city, Mumbai by flight with my parents and reached in the afternoon. As we met on a matrimonial site, his family had already had a formal visit to my city a few weeks before he arrived in India. He came to receive us at the gate and the blood stopped moving in my body. He just gave a smile and I was so nervous that I couldn't even shake my hand with him. I was welcomed at his home with "aarti" and decorations. I felt familiar quickly because I had already met his family before. At that time we finally gave a handshake and laughed at ourselves. It was our eyes that talked and it was sufficient to convey our feelings. Within a few days we got engaged and married.

Mindful Mantras:

- People don't consider LDR as a real relationship. The day you meet is a victory in successfully managing a LDR and a living proof of a relationship. So celebrate!
- The valuable time spent with your partner will become a memory to give you strength to fight against the long distance until you meet your partner again next time. So collect as many photos as you can.
- The strange feeling for the first meeting in LDR is temporary, trust me it will eventually vanish and you will behave normally.

The Garden Of Sunflower

The glorious flowers,
As they bloom with grace,
Glowing bright in the morning's beam,
Setting up a field of thousands of suns,
Landed on the earth,
Shining with hope and pride,
That's where I'll be waiting for you.

Determined to stay tall,
Even in the darkest days,
To find the sunshine and my own way.
Then, converge with you in the middle,
To hold your hand,
And write our story together,
In the garden of sunflower,
That's where I'll be waiting for you.

The Angel Soul

She's beautiful, she's vibrant,
The shiny crystal of the morning dew,
Soothes me, with her kind heart,
She's my angel soul.

He's charming, he's magnificent,
The beaming ray of sunshine,
Brightens me with his gentleness
He's my angel soul.

She's cute, she's confident,
The splashing floral colors of blossom,
Motivates me, to look at the sky,
She's my angel soul.

He's humorous, he's righteous,
The sparkle of the shimmering moon,
Teaches me, to walk through the life,
He's my angel soul.

From here on relationships are seen as general and anyone in a romantic relationship (either long distance or close-by relationships) can relate and overcome the hurdles in the path of life and always support each other as lovers.

The meaning of the following chapters is to encourage couples to understand both happy and sad moments as they progress into their lives and end up making stories as happy couples to pass on to generations ahead.

Just Married

The Vows

Vows simply means commitment which I'll talk about in the next chapter. The reason to mention this chapter on vows is just to make couples conscious about where they stand on the day of marriage. I know the excitement and the strong feelings that fill your hearts when you see dreams changing into reality. During this transition where two souls are finally uniting, couples take wedding vows which are lifetime promises to be there for each other.

"....in sickness and in health....", support each other through the illnesses. (Do the chores, take care of health, you might have some sleepless nights, motivate your partner, heal with love). There is no backing out when one of the partners is ailing.

"....for richer, for poorer....", support your partner in a financial crisis even when you marry them rich. Gather the courage to face the unexpected setbacks and build your empire again. Love is the strongest motivation.

"....to have and to hold...."make a promise to accept your partner unconditionally and stay loyal to each other forever....."till death do us part".

Similarly, in Indian culture, couples take 7 vows to fulfill their respective roles, pray to have prosperous future, protect and stay loyal to each other, be lifelong companions, support each other in all the endeavors, to trust and respect each other's wishes, to stand by each other and to walk on the spiritual path together not only in this life but many lives ahead.

The purpose of writing these vows here is to encourage you to hold on to your relationship no matter how hard it gets because it's a promise to make it worth it in the end. Believe in the magic of two souls uniting on the day of marriage. Whenever tough times arrive in your lives remember these vows, because maybe one of them would surely help you make it through the hurdles. Mainly remember you took these vows because you love your partner. You can also make your own vows in a simpler language to dedicate it to your partner.

Have you thought of some special personalized vows? Write it below and make your partner happy.

1. ____
   ____

2. ____
   ____

3. ____
   ____

"I Do"

I am so lucky,
To have a willing heart to hold.
You came into my life,
Asked for my hand,
To create a fairytale.
To pray together in hard times.
To play together in madness.
To work together for our dreams.
To be a smile on sad days.
To be a medicine for sickness.
To recite our story of growing old together.
I take you as,
The heartbeats of my heart,
The sight to my eyes,
The sound to my voice,
The sweetness to my lips,
The angel of my life.
To the kind soul,
" I Do".

Understanding the Importance of Commitment

Commitment itself means sticking in during good and bad times. It helps couples stay happy even in tough times. Commitment helps you understand your partner better. This trains your mind not to lose patience or faith in your relationship. Moreover, when we talk about long distance relationships it's solely based on trust, love and commitment.

Commitment is a simple but important element in daily lives just like brushing your teeth. You are continuously sticking to your partner subconsciously. The chemistry in a relationship tends to fade with time or the honeymoon phase doesn't stay longer, but commitment is a continuous never ending process. It has the power to re-energize the romantic relationship.

One important aspect for commitment is forgiveness. Once I saw a patient in a cancer hospital, when I went there as a relative of mine was admitted. In the recovery room, patients were being brought from the surgery room. One of the male patients in the recovery room was just coming out of general anesthesia and his wife was standing beside him holding his hand. The patient had a severe habit of chewing tobacco and was suffering from stage 3 mouth cancer. He just got married a few years back and didn't have any children yet. I had talked with that family before surgery. His wife shared with me that she insisted on her husband to leave the tobacco chewing habit but he didn't listen even when he had started developing adverse symptoms. The lady was quite sad and seemed troubled by her husband's attitude. They were from a remote village and they brought her husband to this hospital when he developed some more severe symptoms. The man was diagnosed with cancer and surgical removal of the tumor was done. When he opened his eyes after surgery he found his wife standing right beside him, caressing him and holding his hand as she wasn't able to see him in pain. The first thing that man did was join hands in front of his wife. He literally apologized. The whole hospital staff was astonished by this moment. The man's eyes were clearly resentful. His wife had definitely forgiven him a lot earlier because she had decided to stand by him no matter what. People definitely realize one's importance in their tough times. The man's wife was a true example of commitment. She believed in the power of healing her love and forgiving his partner for his mistakes.

So, commitment is the foundation of a strong relationship. No matter if you leave one relationship and enter another, as soon as the honeymoon phase passes away, the only thing that keeps you going is commitment. Hence don't search for greener grass elsewhere and try to establish the most powerful ways to stick to your partner.

A Promise and A Wish

With a great faith,
I am taken or given,
Where the words are straight,
Bonds are woven.... I am PROMISE.

In the moonlight silence,
I am with lovely solitude,
A shooting star from distance,
In closed eyes from gratitude.... I am WISH.

In the wedding vows,
And the dominion pledge,
The trust tied in bows,
And time has no edge.... I am PROMISE.

In this eternal universe,
I reside in purity,
I am the medium to converse,
With the God almighty.... I am WISH.

"I am bound with two substances, and taken care of ".... Said promise.
"I am a supernatural demand, residing freely within a soul ".... Said wish.
"I am the proud moment ".... Said promise.
"I am the divine belief ".... Said wish.

You jump, I jump

The distance that parts us,
Waiting for the time zones,
Long time to meet up,
Teary eyes through the screen.

Some days of sickness,
Or may be of crisis,
The events of sadness,
Or the pain to endure.

No matter what,
I assure you that,
We'd be there for us,
Holding our hands.

Pain and Medicine

Relationships do have moments of pain. Pain caused due to arguments, or some critical situation in life. There is pain in love but love is also the medicine to any kind of emotional pain. What I mean to explain here is, when life gives you a moment of pain, have faith in your love for your partner. No matter how bad the situation is, love is the cure.

Let me explain it with an example. Few couples who were divorced, or were on the verge of divorce, or were having an unhealthy relationship were taken into counseling about their relationship. When they were asked to speak about their first meeting, honeymoon, or holding their child in their hands for the first time, everyone had a smile on their face, or would be lost in their thoughts while sharing that they forget their current pain. So in any relationship, the love is actually vanishing because it's associated with some bitter experience. Love actually is an element that never dies. Love has the potential to cure the problems of the relationship.

If both the couples leave their fears, resentment and egos aside and remember why and how they started their romantic relationship, it would first remove some bitterness and tension between both partners. Then give a chance to your love, trust in its potential. Love is the biggest cure in the universe. Instead of blaming, take charge of your relationship and see how you start dealing with difficult situations together. Like it's well said that life isn't a bed of roses and hence tough times are unavoidable part of life. Once you trust your love and learn to keep going on in life by holding your partner's hand, you'll remember this time in your old age.

Make this the mantra of your life,

Love, Love and Love….

We are born to love and spread love.

Into Your Eyes

I search the comfort paths,
At the end of the day,
Heart filled with endless faith,
Only place I like to stay,
When I look into your eyes....

In the eternal shine,
Clear as winter night sky,
As the strings of heart twine,
Take me to heaven so high,
When I look into your eyes....

All the shades of marbles,
Are spread so wide,
Mesmerized with infinite colors,
Withholding me by your side,
When I look into your eyes....

With the depths of nature,
Whether joy or sorrow,
It feels marvelous adventure,
As I get a glimpse of tomorrow,
When I look into your eyes....

The Scars

Like the bright moon,
Full of light,
Beautiful even with its scars,
Shines brilliant,
In the silent night.

The scars of life,
Hidden deep into the hearts,
Of innumerable mankind,
Each has a story to tell,
Of the healing wounds.

The wounds of loss,
Of person or a part,
The holes in the heart,
Pain in the periphery,
Living through the dark nights.

The time will pour in,
Through these holes,
Hidden cure in your soul,
Will heal and lift you up,
From the heaps of sorrow.

Hope will discover you,
And make you shine brighter,
The light will shower again,
Just as the beautiful moon,
With the scars.

Senescence

According to me, one of the most beautiful moments of a successful relationship is seeing couples cherish the essence of their relationship in their old age. I believe that senescence does mean deterioration of body cells functions with age but it doesn't signify the diminishing love. I have seen old couples holding hands, dancing in the rain, giving each other their shoulders to cry on and fulfill lifetime promises.

If lovers target to grow into such couples, their life gets a precious goal to achieve. Each love story that reaches the peak at old age is a story to pass on to generations to come. The successful couples that make it to old age, are often those who change their perspectives of life. They tend to visualize life in a positive way and focus towards their betterment. They easily accept the changes and give emotional meaning to it. Old age narrows the vision to focus on the remaining time they have and make out most of it. It's the age where you aren't loving your partner because of their beauty but you are in love with the precious soul of your partner, which never gets old, until your last breath.

Let me give you a simple example of how mature love is at old age. Once I was traveling in a bus and an old couple was sitting behind my seat. When the bus took a few minutes to halt at a restaurant, the old man was climbing down the bus to get some food. He asked his wife what she would like to eat and she replied to bring her potato chips. The old man first asked which brand of chips, then he asked which flavor and how spicy. The old lady replied and the man left to bring the chips. I looked at that lady and she gave me a smile. This gave me courage to interrogate her whether her husband always takes care of her food like this. The lady replied that she and her husband have traveled alone many times and everytime he would ask without fail, what she would like to eat, which flavors, brands, toppings, cuisine she would like to have. He takes care of all the specifications of food, be it ice cream, cake, or any other food items. I appreciated this old couple as asking such basic questions is very definite in initial phases of a relationship or dating but seeing it reach till old age was fascinating to me.

Moreover, if one surpasses the hurdles of long distance relationships and make it till old age then it's the most heavenly experience and definitely a role model for the generations to come. So I advise you to look around the experienced, mature lovers, the old couples. Learn from them and take their guidance for successful relationships and most importantly, share and discuss with your partner to imbibe those values in your relationship too.

Life is a continuous learning process and so is love.

Keep learning, Keep loving !

With your blessings, I hope to write the revised edition of this book a few years later with some more of my real life experiences until old age and how long distance strengthened our relationship when we finally started living together.

May God bless everyone.

The Soul: Without Wrinkles

Where to lead,
Confused, I stare,
Here in front of
Mirror, I stand.

In utter amazement,
I ask the perfect crystals,
The principle of time,
And the questions of life.

'Mirror, mirror, on the wall,
Who's the most honest of them all?'
"Oh Dear, it's an expensive gift,
Hand in hand with trust indeed,
Don't expect it from anyone unless
You can rely with closed eyes on them."

'Mirror, mirror on the wall,
Who's the most loyal of them all?'
"Oh Dear, it's a fair test,
Very precious and attractive of all,
Any wealth can't build it up,
As it's the faith that takes it all."

'Mirror, mirror on the wall,
Who's the genius of them all?'
"Oh dear, I doubt the fact,
They are the ones to find,
The answer to the soft and strong,
Each human can be a genius after all."

'Mirror, mirror on the wall,
Who's the loveliest of them all?'
"Oh dear, I have seen millions of faces,
All I do is dive deep in their soul,
Face is not that is lovely after all,
It's the inner self that beautifies you as a whole."

Bliss of Love

Today as the drops of rain,
Touch my skin,
I feel your spirit,
Touch my soul.
Reminding me of the rain dances,
As u spin me around,
To the graceful movements,
Your presence rejuvenates the moment.

Later the sun shines,
The rays showering hope,
And as I am bathed in sunlight,
All glowing golden,
Reminding me of the mornings,
When you gave me smooches,
To greet me good day,
And be grateful to have you by my side.

As twilight approaches,
The wondrous night flows,
Slowing down the pace,
And the living beings, snoozing off.
Reminding me of the evening walks,
Where you hold my hand,
Giving me a promise,
That I'll never face the world alone.

Into the night,
When the world goes into rest,
In the deep slumber,
And into eternal peace.
Reminding me of the stargazing,
With your arms around me,
The best place I can ever have,
To look upon another morning.

Recipe of LDR

Patience,
Trust,
Time,
Loyalty,
And Love,
Are the chief ingredients.
Add to it,
A spoonful of care,
A cup of respect,
A quart of empathy,
A tablespoon of voice mails,
A handful of FaceTime dates
And humor to taste.
Let it ripen with love and care.
Finally, garnish it with,
Wedding vows
And lifetime promises,
To grow old together.

If this book made a positive impact on your long distance relationship or saved your relationships (be it long distance or close-by relationship), then you may write to me on the email address below and do share your experience.

I believe every relationship is a unique one and if you want to share your story you are most welcomed. Please drop your story in the email address below. I would surely respond as soon as possible.

If you want to use my poetries (or any content of this book) in any form (as simple as dedicating it to your partner), please take prior permission by dropping an email to the below address as all the contents in this book are subject to copyright. Copyright infringement can lead to legal actions.

Contact: namuhelpsldr@gmail.com

http://www.namratasantoki.in

Printed by Libri Plureos GmbH in Hamburg, Germany

9 789357 042901